THE LIFE OF TU FU

Eliot Weinberger

A New Directions Paperbook Original

Some of these poems first appeared in *Poetry*, *The Paris Review*, and *Voice and Verse* (Hong Kong)—thanks to editors Srikanth Reddy and Tammy Lai-Ming Ho.

Manufactured in the United States of America
First published as a New Directions Paperbook (NDP1595) in 2024

Library of Congress Cataloging-in-Publication Data
Names: Weinberger, Eliot, author.
Title: The life of Tu Fu / Eliot Weinberger.
Description: First edition. | New York, NY: New Directions Publishing Corporation, 2024.
Identifiers: LCCN 2023045524 | ISBN 9780811238052 (paperback) | ISBN 9780811238069 (ebook)
Subjects: LCSH: Du, Fu, 712–770—Poetry. | LCGFT: Biographical poetry.
Classification: LCC PS3573.E3928 L54 2024 | DDC 811/.54—dc23/eng/20231013
LC record available at https://lccn.loc.gov/2023045524

10 9 8 7 6 5 4 3 2 1

New Directions Books are published for James Laughlin
by New Directions Publishing Corporation
80 Eighth Avenue, New York 10011

ndbooks.com

THE LIFE OF TU FU

They say this is the only tree in the world that has these pears, for these pears have no desire to propagate elsewhere.

I thought of The Old Man Who Called His Chickens. He had hundreds of chickens, each with its own name. He could call its name and the chicken would come. I thought of him when all the candidates, including me, failed the exam.

In the Eastern Capital it is tiring being clever.

Chanting poems in the Hall of Gathering Kingfisher Feathers, drinking in the Pavilion for Gazing at Clouds.

They only talk about plum blossoms and never notice the new shoots of a willow.

There are plums and melons and pears and grapes, but they love lychees, for lychees come from far away.

The flowers here make everyone crazy.
Better to be with bamboo.

On either side of me, people take strong positions and never agree.

I have a hard time remembering what anyone says.

I thought of the poet Hsi K'ang, who was often told that he was talented but unwise. Just before he was executed, he wrote the poem "Now I Am Ashamed."

They say that at the entrance to a house one can always be hit by a falling roof tile.

These days I'm already sad before I get drunk and drunk I have no place to go.

I tug at my robe but it still won't cover my shins.

Too poor for a horse, at least I have feet.

In the palace, there's camel-hoof stew and tangerines.

I thought of Wang Hsien-chi. When thieves broke into his house, he asked them not to take his old green rug.

They say immortals eat cloud-seed rice, which is shattered mica.

The music stops; moonlight shines on the planks of the floor.

Send me a letter.

There are no men left; they're conscripting boys.

The chubby ones have mothers saying goodbye; the thin ones just look forlorn.

Everyone has cousins who died in the war.

I remember, when we were kids, you were better than me at counting coins.

He said: "At fifteen you're sent north to guard the river; at forty you're sent west to the forts. Those who make it back home have gray hair; the rest are bones in some field."

Half the people of Ch'in are now the wandering ghosts of the unburied. In the abandoned villages, the new ghosts are in torment and the old ghosts weep for them.

He said: "To kill a man, I'm taught, first shoot the horse. I watch the clouds, but can't follow them away."

An abandoned courtyard: an old tree:
A temple bell lying on its side:
The world I live in.

They win and we lose; we lose and they win.
Vines wrap around the rotting bones.

She knows he won't come back from the army, but
patches the clothes he left just in case.

In the street a woman is weeping.
A boy walks by whistling.
An officer changes his horse.
The clouds are brown and unmoving.
The wind picks up.

All things do what they do:
Birds swoop to catch an insect.
Moonlight breaks through the forest leaves.
Soldiers guard the border.
I am trapped in this body.

I lift my face to watch the birds.
I turn my head, thinking someone has called me.

I wrote four poems:
on a sick cypress, on a sick orange tree,
on a withered palm, and a withered nanmu.

You ask how I'm doing:
Listen to the wild geese echoing
and the war horses galloping by.

Even the birds avoid Peach Grove, by the Yellow River.
Only a single cloud looks over the slaughter.

I thought of the scholar Ting Ling-wei from Liaotung,
who mastered the Way and became an immortal crane.
He flew back to the city and perched on the city gate.
Young men tried to shoot at him with arrows. He flew
high into the air and sang:

> *The walls of the city are the same,*
> *but the people are different.*
> *Better to become an immortal.*

When I see snow on the pines, I'll get a boat out of here.

By day, sailing past abandoned villages.
Snow still on the sunken rooftops.
Somewhere it's spring.

I saw a sick eagle, almost featherless on a leafless willow.
The fishermen complain their nets have frozen.

At night, anchored, I hear a horn from somewhere.
North of here: the war horses.

Day breaks; darkness fades; the stars thin out;
the snow lets up;
magpies on the towers and crowds of crows take off;
the river barely moves along the city walls:
it will take a long time to go home.

Thousands of white-headed ravens on Redbird Gate.
Trees barely visible in the fog; only the sound of the gar-
rison drums.

Impossible to know if the news is just rumor:
Officials, they say, are disguising themselves as fishermen
and butchers.

Rebels ride the horses of ghosts.
Why do they always burn things down?

I thought of that Immortal who lived in a world inside
a clay pot.

Here the men sit and the women stand; the men stay home and the women climb the mountains, collecting firewood.

The landscape is beautiful, the weather terrible, and they call their temple Taking Poison.

In these mountains I imagine I hear
bears and leopards and tigers and baboons,
but all I see is a man on a ladder,
cutting bamboo.

No news; snow whirls.
In the street, the bones of the frozen.

A hut with a single window made from the broken rim
of a large pot.

For three months, the beacon fires of the rebels in the
mountains.
The East Wind smells like blood.

I remember when ordinary people were merely distrustful.
Birds keep themselves hidden, but sing.

There are cuckoos in West Sichuan but no cuckoos in East Sichuan.
There are cuckoos in Yunnan but no cuckoos in Fuzhou.
They say when a cuckoo cries it sounds like the words "You should go home."

Friends with good jobs have stopped writing.

Here the houses are impressive, there are crowds and music in the streets.
I don't know a soul.

In the shade of a mulberry I just stand and look at the bridge.
No one walks by the river.

Wind in the bamboo, foam from the river on the sand.
What news from the capital? I hear the cavalry's retreated.

So dark I eat dinner at breakfast.
So rainy I imagine the mountain washing away.
The downpour so strong fish in the river sank.
The mud so bad I was sorry I asked you over.

The world is damp and dry, damp or dry.
Two swallows suddenly came into my room.
They were raised in dust and wind.
It took them a long time to get here,
escaping the damp and dry of the world like me.

A single petal falling means less spring.
A kingfisher's nest, a dragonfly's wing:
Study closely the patterns of things.

The mind is crystal.
Rain soaks my clothes.

Soldiers still guard the ruined palace: rats run across the tiles.

A squirrel with folded hands outside his broken nest.

That dandelion in the wind once had roots.

Live like a wren, unnoticed on a high branch, and you'll stay alive.

It's been so many years: I imagine her face, looking at me skeptically.

Mushrooms grow on the collapsed temple columns. Painted dragons peel off the walls.

I thought of Lien P'o: when he was general, the troops slept late.

I thought of the Han Emperor T'ai Tsung, who never killed those who criticized him.

I thought of the magistrate Fan Tan, who was so honest his steamer was covered in dust.

I thought of Fu-tzu Chien: when he was administrator of Shanfu, he spent the whole time playing the zither and the city was well governed.

What does a wren think when the sun goes down?

Wandering for ten years, trying to alight on one safe branch.
I open my trunk and stare at the clothes.

Moonlight on old clothes.
Old clothes and the same old crows.

I thought of the philosopher Yang Chu, who always wept when he came to a fork in the road.

Plants with thorns only seem to grow where people walk.

The people in these parts are strange.
They're unfriendly to old friends and unfriendlier to
those they've just met.

They raise cormorants at home and every day they just
eat sturgeon.
You can't trust them either.

The roosters crow long after the sun rises.
There's thunder in the cold of winter.

I thought of Confucius, who said that if a unicorn is ever
actually captured, no one will know what it is.

A boat abandoned in a whirlpool in the Wu Gorges; kingfisher feathers swirling around it.

I thought of Wen Ch'iao, mooring his boat at Ox Island. Knowing there were invisible water demons around, he burned a rhinoceros horn to make them visible. But invisible water demons want to be unseen, and they killed him.

Last autumn I saw some soldier gallop by,
his lance under his arm.
And now I suddenly wonder,
where his white bones lie.
Every day whole regiments die,
and everyone weeps, one corpse at a time.

Moon through the latticework.
Can't sleep. I walk the shadows on the floor.

I thought of Liu K'un. Surrounded by enemy troops, late at night he climbed a tower and played sad songs on a reed pipe. The soldiers, overcome with homesickness, abandoned their posts and the city was saved.

Huge fish hide under the waves.

At dawn in the green mud,
at dusk in the green mud,
at noon passing a deer who died
stuck in the green mud.

I dread that I'll die by the side of the road, and only be
remembered for that.

Why do stupidities become customs?

I thought of those monkeys who were furious that they were given three acorns in the morning and four at night; so their keeper gave them four in the morning and three at night and they were peaceful again.

Parrots are more intelligent than people: they know they're in a cage.

Better to go back to sleep.

Mt. Wu lit by the moon.
Who put the stars up there?

I thought of the story of the blind man in the *Nirvana Sutra*. A doctor shaved his eyeballs with a golden scalpel and cured him, but he did not know how to see.

They say failure in early life will bring success at the end,
but birds know when they're tired of flying,
and clouds have no will of their own.

I scratch my head and knock out a hairpin,
more concerned with medicines than poetry.

Around here no one does a thing.
Even minor clerks are surly towards me.

A desolate terrace in the wind; cliffs above; a ravine below, fog hovering over the river.
A single goose in the clouds, unnoticed by the crows.
Boulders on the verge of rolling down.

They say that travelers weep when a gibbon, hanging from a branch, cries three times.

There's no end to the insincere: why bother to mention them?

Deep in this valley, sunlight is brief and the tax collectors
go home late at night.
The girls pick fiddlehead ferns to sell.

Better to have a daughter who can marry the neighbor;
a son will just end up in the ground.

Letters rarely come.

Even the apes are cold this high in the mountains.
The wind blows the geese out of formation.

At Chen-ti Temple, I asked the Master about the Dharma,
and he said I was deluded writing poetry.

I thought of how, in Han times, poems often began: "A
single cloud in the northwest."

True, my mind moves as slowly as a cloud, but a cloud
moves on.

These days the poets sit on a log and wait for a fish.

Useless medicines strewn around the room:
I keep hearing the sound of wood being chopped when
no one is chopping.

Fireflies sneak in and land on piles of clothes.
Where will I be next year?

I must ask someone to scratch my back.

They beat drums all night; they whip themselves; they burn statues of dragons; they lay a dying man under the sun so that Heaven will take pity, but still no rain.

Soldiers keep wearing their armor in the heat; everyone else stays home, lying down.

I've grown attached to my palm leaf whisk, waving the flies away.

The moon a giant pearl in the blackness.
Will I ever escape rebirth?

I eat in the rain, under the river willows.

I lean on the railing.

I write poems about what I see, for things pass so quickly.

This morning the clouds are thin.
Last night the moon was yellow.

Peach blossoms in the river current; ducks below the dock.
A single seagull, tossed around in the wind.

It is beneath you never to forget petty slights.

When birds call they call to their own kind.
Gibbons hang from the branches and imitate each other.
Gulls stand in a line side by side and think only of them-
selves.

Thirty years since I've seen you and I still see you getting
on the boat.
Ashes smolder in a heart that's died.

They sell their children to pay the taxes.
They hope their counterfeit coins will work.

The army has taken all the horses;
even the officials ride mangy donkeys.

Today is like yesterday.
Troops still on the Central Plain.

They say that when a goose flies south it holds a twig in
its beak to keep from making a sound the hunters might
hear.

The body grows weaker, but gazing at the mountains remains the same.
In the distance, smoke rises from the scattered houses burned by marauders.

Their pennants are the tails of black horses.
Their swords are forged with patterns of stars.

Is there anyone still left, under a leaking roof, looking out the door?
They even killed the chickens and the dogs.

A white horse with two arrows in its empty saddle.

The corpses lying by the road change so much in a single day.

I wish I could talk with someone.

The only people I meet are people I've never known.

I thought of Chuang Tzu: "Be careful not to disturb the human mind."

You'll weep for reasons other than the war.

There's a lot to see on a dead-end road,
but not much kindness.

Bitter bamboo so bitter
insects won't eat it.

Bitter bamboo so low
birds won't nest in it.

Bitter bamboo so weak
it's useless for building.

Bitter bamboo to plant around my hut.

Today I am not happy.
The heart is not a stone that can be rolled.

They say that rocks turn into swallows in the rain, and back to rocks when it clears.

They say that when it rains for seven days, a leopard does not hunt, and cultivates the patterns in its coat.

They say there is a certain thunder clap when a carp turns into a dragon.

They say that a chicken has five virtues: civil talents, military talents, courage, moral rectitude, and fidelity.

They say that when a master archer shoots, his prey drops at the twang of the bowstring.

No one understood when I wrote: "The sun rises from its bath like a duckweed."

The sea accepts the water from all the streams.

The war goes on: I live among deer.
I sit out in the moonlight and moonlight shines on my
knees.
I sit out even when it rains.

I thought of the sage Wang Hui-chih who was appointed
to the Ministry of Mounts. Asked what his duties were,
he said he did not know, but people were always bring-
ing him horses. Asked how many horses, he said a sage
doesn't think about horses.

Watching the horses being washed,
listening to the cicadas in the trees.

I write about what is happening:
I record the dawns and sunsets.

I wonder why cherries are all the same size.

If it is not painted perfectly, a tiger will look like a dog.

An orange tree is so relaxed.

I hadn't seen that cormorant for a long time, but now it's back, looking at me.
It knows what's on my mind.

I thought of the master calligrapher Wang Hsi-chih, who wrote out the whole *Tao Te Ching* and traded it for a goose.

No time to be lazy:
This morning I combed my hair.

I walk around the yard with a small axe:
Things that are useless always flourish.

I go to bed early, I get up so late, how can I do anything?

I must finish that chicken coop.
They're knocking the plates off the table.

The four little pines I planted are choked with vines.
The fish are not biting and the deer just run off and
don't bother to look back.

There's no path to my cottage, but I'd clear one for you.

When melons get ripe in the fall, I think of you in
Melon Village.
How are the melons this year?

Nothing easier than lettuce,
so why doesn't mine grow?

The door rattles in the wind.

I was pretty smart when I was seven.

These poor chrysanthemums took root in the wrong place.
The bean sprouts rotted in the damp and the melons cracked in the frost.

We're the same age—so why do I look so much older?

Even when my teeth have fallen out, I'll still have my tongue.
A carp, flapping in a carriage rut.

It's not that I'm avoiding others;
it's just that there are too many wagons on the road.

I wondered if sparrows no longer twitter,
then realized I'm going deaf.

My mirror is skilled at hurrying old age.
I've given up garlic and scallions.

Drinking now makes me ill, so I'll just watch you,
a little jealous when you fall over.

Why should crickets bring on melancholy?

Life's so short, said Chuang Tzu, it's like watching a white colt run by through a crack in a fence.

I remembered watching Kung-sun in her brocade robes perform the "Sword Dance" when I was a child.

I thought of General Yin Hao, who lost a battle and was demoted to a commoner. He spent the rest of his days writing the same two characters over and over in the air with his finger: HOW STRANGE.

Your letter came: you're alive.

As for me, I've achieved nothing.
My shoes have turned green and my hat blows off in the wind.

I wobble even where the ground is flat.
When my coffin closes that will be the end of that.

I thought of Chiang Yen who dreamed that Kuo P'o, long dead, appeared and asked for his writing brush back, and after he awoke Chiang Yen never wrote poems again.

I thought of Tsu Yung who, at his examination, wrote a poem of only four lines. Questioned by the examiner, he replied: "That was all I had to say."

The moon, the river, the boat, an egret, a fish, a splash, a lamp rocking in the wind.

This is not a translation of individual poems, but a fictional autobiography of Tu Fu derived and adapted from the thoughts, images, and allusions in the poetry.

In the 13th century, the resistance fighter Wen T'ien-hsiang, imprisoned during the Mongol conquest of the Southern Sung Dynasty, wrote (as translated by Lucas Bender):

> As I sat in prison in Yu Yen, I had nothing to do and chanted Tu Fu's poems. Having become somewhat familiar with the feelings and inspirations they contained, I took his five-character lines and compiled them into quatrains. After some time at this, I had gotten two hundred such quatrains. Everything I had to say had already been said for me by Tu Fu.

While Wen T'ien-hsiang's intention was to produce patriotic and inspirational verses, and he, of course, reproduced the rearranged lines exactly in Chinese, the process here has been similar. For "prison" in the passage above, read "the pandemic." For "Yu Yen," read "New York." For "chanted," read "read." For "quatrains," read "montages." For "two hundred such quatrains," read "fifty-eight poems."

ELIOT WEINBERGER'S books of literary essays include *Karmic Traces*, *An Elemental Thing*, *The Ghosts of Birds*, and *Angels & Saints*. His political writings are collected in *What I Heard About Iraq* and *What Happened Here: Bush Chronicles*. The author of a study of Chinese poetry translation, *Nineteen Ways of Looking at Wang Wei*, he is a translator of the poetry of Bei Dao, the editor of *The New Directions Anthology of Classical Chinese Poetry*, and the general editor of the series *Calligrams: Writings from and on China*. Among his translations of Latin American poetry and prose are *The Poems of Octavio Paz*, Paz's *In Light of India*, Vicente Huidobro's *Altazor*, Xavier Villaurrutia's *Nostalgia for Death*, and Jorge Luis Borges's *Seven Nights and Selected Non-Fictions*. His work has been translated into over thirty languages, and he has been publishing with New Directions since 1975.